I0418585

The Principal's Art of War

Strategic Leadership for Schools Under Pressure

Darren L Avent Sr

Copyright © 2025 by Darren L Avent Sr.

All rights reserved.

No portion of this book may be reproduced in any form without written permission from the publisher or author, except as permitted by U.S. copyright law.

This publication is designed to provide accurate and authoritative information in regard to the subject matter covered. It is sold with the understanding that neither the author nor the publisher is engaged in rendering legal, investment, accounting or other professional services. While the publisher and author have used their best efforts in preparing this book, they make no representations or warranties with respect to the accuracy or completeness of the contents of this book and specifically disclaim any implied warranties of merchantability or fitness for a particular purpose. No warranty may be created or extended by sales representatives or written sales materials. The advice and strategies contained herein may not be suitable for your situation. You should consult with a professional when appropriate. Neither the publisher nor the author shall be liable for any loss of profit or any other commercial damages, including but not limited to special, incidental, consequential, personal, or other damages.

NOTE ON SOURCES Quotations from Sun Tzu's The Art of War are drawn from Lionel Giles' 1910 translation (public domain). Some passages are paraphrased to clarify application to modern school leadership contexts.

DEDICATION

For the principals in the trenches— the ones carrying entire communities on their backs and still showing up with heart.

For my mother, Doris— whose careful eye helped polish these words into something worthy of the leaders who'll read them.

And for my wife, Charita— whose love, support, and patience gave me the strength to finish this work.

This book is for all of you.

Contents

Introduction
The Battlefield Called School

It's 8:45 AM on a Tuesday, and I'm standing in the main hallway of a middle school watching 700 students flood through the doors. Backpacks slung over shoulders. AirPods in ears. Energy—chaotic, unpredictable, alive—filling every corner of the building.

In twenty minutes, the bell will ring. Classes will start. The building will quiet down. But right now, it's controlled chaos. And I'm watching it with the same calm I used to watch a convoy roll through uncertain terrain.

Command presence. That's what they called it in the military. The ability to stand in the middle of chaos and project calm, control, and confidence—even when you don't have all the answers. Especially when you don't have all the answers.

A fight breaks out near the lockers. Two students, shoving, voices rising. I move—not running, not frantic—just moving with purpose. By the time I get there, a teacher has already stepped between them. I position myself to de-escalate, separate, and redirect. Thirty seconds later, both students are walking to the office with me. Calm. No spectacle. No drama.

Another principal might have seen a discipline problem. I saw a tactical situation: terrain (crowded hallway), time (bell about to ring), resources (teacher already engaged), objective (separate, de-escalate, maintain order without escalating tension). I didn't think it through consciously. It was instinct. Military instinct applied to a middle school hallway.

That's what this book is about.

This is not a how-to manual. It's a way of thinking.

If you're looking for scripts, checklists, or quick fixes, this isn't that book. If you want to think more clearly under pressure, lead without burning out, and stop fighting losing battles—keep reading.

Not turning schools into boot camps. Not treating students like soldiers or teachers like subordinates. But recognizing that the principles of strategy, leadership, and tactical thinking that have guided military leaders for thousands of years apply just as powerfully to the complex, high-stakes, resource-constrained world of school leadership.

And no one understood strategy better than Sun Tzu.

Sun Tzu was a Chinese general who lived about 2,500 years ago. His book, *The Art of War*, is the most influential text on strategy ever written. Why? Because Sun Tzu figured out something that applies whether you're commanding armies or leading schools: **the smartest leaders win by thinking strategically, not by fighting harder.**

His principles aren't about warfare. They're about reading situations, building alliances, conserving resources, and shaping outcomes before battles even begin. In a profession where you're constantly competing—for funding, staff, enrollment, community trust—strategic thinking isn't optional. It's survival.

From the Marine Corps to the Principal's Office

I didn't start my career in education. I started it in the United States Marine Corps, where I served eight years as an Amphibious Assault Vehicle Crewman, deploying to Desert Shield and Desert Storm. I reached the rank of Corporal, learning what leadership looks like when the stakes are life and death and the mission depends on every person executing under pressure.

After the Marines, I commissioned as an Infantry Officer in the Army National Guard. They paid for my teaching credential—which is how I ended up in a Newark, New Jersey high school classroom, then as an administrator, and eventually as a principal in Oakland, California.

The transition from military service to school leadership taught me something critical: the principles of strategic thinking don't change, only the context.

In the military, we learned to plan before acting, build alliances before needing them, prepare systems before crises hit, and lead with calm when everything was falling apart. Those same principles—applied differently, executed with care—transformed struggling schools into thriving ones.

At Kaiser Elementary, I walked into a school with broken morale, a demoralized staff, and a culture of distrust. Three years later, it was thriving. At Montera Middle School, I led an eight-year transformation that included IB training, block scheduling, and a complete cultural shift. During COVID, I navigated remote learning without losing my staff or my students.

I didn't do it by working harder. I did it by winning smarter.

And the framework I used? Sun Tzu's Art of War.

What This Book Will Teach You

Traditional school leadership advice tells you to work harder, stay positive, and build relationships. That's not wrong. But it's incomplete.

Without strategy, even the most dedicated leaders burn out, fail, or leave the profession.

This book will teach you to:

Build alliances with people who initially oppose you

Navigate crises with calm and clarity

Create systems that function under pressure

Lead effectively even when you're an outsider

Protect your people from burnout while maintaining high standards

Know when to fight and when to find another way

The examples are real. The challenges are real. The strategies work.

Who This Book Is For

This book is for:

New principals overwhelmed by the complexity and politics of the job

Assistant principals preparing for the principalship and wanting to think strategically

Veteran principals who are burned out and looking for a smarter way to lead

District leaders and coaches supporting school leaders with frameworks that actually work

If you've ever felt like you're fighting a war you can't win, this book is for you.

If you've ever wondered why leadership feels so exhausting, this book is for you.

If you've ever thought, There has to be a better way to do this, this book is for you.

The Promise

By the end of this book, you'll have a new way of thinking about school leadership. You'll stop seeing every problem as a battle to fight and start seeing opportunities to maneuver, adapt, and win strategically.

Sun Tzu wrote: "Supreme excellence consists in breaking the enemy's resistance without fighting."

In schools, the "enemy" isn't people. It's chaos, dysfunction, burnout, and the systems that fail our students. And the way we defeat those forces isn't by working ourselves to death—it's by thinking strategically, leading wisely, and building the capacity of everyone around us.

True leadership isn't about fighting harder.

It's about winning smarter.

Now you'll learn how.

Laying Plans
Strategy and Vision

The Wisdom of Sun Tzu

"The general who wins a battle makes many calculations in his temple before the battle is fought. The general who loses a battle makes but few calculations beforehand."

"If you know the enemy and know yourself, you need not fear the result of a hundred battles."

Interpretation: Strategy Before Action

Sun Tzu's first principle is deceptively simple: plan before you act.

But planning isn't making lists or setting goals. It's strategic analysis. It's asking: What are we really fighting? What do we have that others don't? What battle can we actually win?

In the military, rushed decisions based on incomplete information get people killed. The commanders who survived—and won—studied the situation thoroughly, anticipated problems, and built plans that accounted for multiple contingencies.

School leadership demands the same discipline. You will face threats: enrollment decline, competition from charters, budget cuts, shifting demographics. The principal who reacts impulsively loses ground. The principal who studies the problem, understands the competition, and builds a multi-year strategy has a chance.

Here's the harder truth: strategic planning requires patience. It requires saying "not yet" when everyone wants action now. It requires building coalitions, securing resources, and laying groundwork before you announce anything publicly.

The battle is won or lost long before the first move is made.

At Montera Middle School, I faced a threat that traditional responses couldn't solve. So I spent a year planning a strategy that would redefine what our school stood for.

Real-World Example: The Threat We Couldn't Ignore

When I became principal of Montera Middle School, we were losing students.

Not catastrophically, not overnight—but steadily, year after year, families were choosing a tech charter school we'll call Horizon Academy instead of us.

Horizon Academy promised personalized learning through technology. Every student got a Chromebook. Lessons were individualized. Progress was tracked digitally. For families who believed the future was tech-driven, Horizon Academy felt like the smarter choice.

And we were bleeding enrollment.

The previous administration had tried to respond. We bought Chromebooks. We implemented online learning platforms. We talked about personalized learning.

Families still left.

We were trying to compete on Horizon Academy's terms. We couldn't win that battle. We needed to differentiate, not imitate.

Know Yourself, Know the Enemy

Sun Tzu's teaching is clear: if you know the enemy and know yourself, you need not fear the result of a hundred battles.

So I studied both.

I studied Horizon Academy. What were they offering that we weren't? Technology, yes. But more than that—a vision of the future. A narrative that said, "The world is digital. Your child needs to be fluent in technology to succeed. We provide that."

It was compelling. And it was working.

Then I studied us. What did we have that Horizon Academy didn't? What could we offer that they couldn't replicate?

The answer wasn't technology. We had Chromebooks too. But we weren't going to out-tech a school whose entire identity was built around technology.

And that's when the strategy became clear: we couldn't win the tech battle. But we could win the "whole child" battle.

Horizon Academy was all screens, all digital, all individualized learning through computers. What if we went the opposite direction? What if we brought back the things technology was replacing—art, music, hands-on learning, human connection?

What if we became the school that said, "Yes, technology matters. But so does creativity, collaboration, and building things with your hands"?

That became our strategy. Not to compete with Horizon Academy. To offer something they couldn't.

The Plan: A Three-Year Strategy

I didn't announce this at a staff meeting in September and expect it to happen by January. Strategic change takes time.

We built a three-year plan.

Year 1: Laying the groundwork.

I approached the superintendent with a bold idea: send our teachers to International Baccalaureate (IB) training. IB focuses on inquiry-based learning, critical thinking, and developing well-rounded students. We couldn't afford full IB authorization—and that wasn't the goal. The goal was IB-style training to deepen instruction.

The superintendent believed in the vision. He agreed to fund the training—not to become an IB school, but to elevate our instructional quality and give teachers a framework for deeper, more rigorous teaching.

That year, we trained. We studied. We learned what it meant to teach students how to think, not just what to think. And we started building the culture that would support the larger changes coming.

Year 2: Developing the plan.

We couldn't just add art and music classes and hope families noticed. We needed a structural change—something bold enough to signal that Montera was different.

I visited a high school in our district using a block schedule. Instead of six 50-minute periods every day, they ran four 75-minute periods on an A/B rotation. Students had four classes one day, four different classes the next day.

The benefits were clear:

Deeper instruction (75 minutes allowed teachers to go beyond surface-level content)

Fewer transitions (four classes instead of six, reducing chaos)

Room for electives (space for art, music, foreign language without cutting core academics)

No middle school in our district had tried this. But I knew it could work.

I also knew I needed staff buy-in. So I brought the idea to teachers. I listened to concerns. The biggest one was immediate: "We'll lose our prep time."

They were right. On an A/B schedule, teachers wouldn't have prep every day.

So I made a deal: One day, you have your own prep—time that's yours to plan, grade, and breathe. The other day, you have collaborative prep where you meet as a department to plan together, share strategies, and build curriculum.

The collaborative prep wasn't a loss—it was an investment in better teaching. And it gave teachers a voice in shaping how the schedule would work.

By the end of Year 2, we had the framework. Block schedule. Required arts and music. Foreign language for all students. And a commitment to hands-on, experiential learning.

Year 3: Implementation.

We launched the new schedule. We hired new art and music teachers. We expanded our woodshop program by hiring a teacher who'd attended Montera as a student, taken woodshop, and become a professional woodworker.

Under his leadership, students weren't making birdhouses. They were building real, functional furniture—chairs, tables, pieces we could sell at fundraisers.

We became the first middle school in the district to implement a block schedule—not as a gimmick, but as the backbone of our whole-child strategy. And we made it clear to families: Montera is the school that develops the whole student—academically, creatively, and practically.

The Execution: Making the Vision Real

The transition wasn't seamless. Change never is.

Teachers were skeptical. The collaborative prep felt like a loss of autonomy at first. Some worried that 75-minute periods would be harder to manage. Others questioned whether we were sacrificing academic rigor for "soft" electives.

But I didn't force compliance. I invited collaboration.

Teachers helped design the collaborative prep structure. Department chairs shaped how their teams would use that time. And as the year progressed, teachers started to see the benefits: deeper lessons, stronger relationships with students, and the ability to actually finish a unit without the bell constantly interrupting.

Sixth graders explored both art and music—a semester of each—before choosing one to focus on in 7th and 8th grade. This prevented the "I picked the wrong one" regret.

The woodshop became legendary. Students made real things. They took pride in their work. Parents came to open houses and saw their kids' furniture displayed like gallery pieces.

The block schedule worked. Teachers adapted. Students adjusted. And within a semester, it felt normal.

The Results: Differentiation, Not Imitation

By the end of Year 3, the results were undeniable.

Enrollment stabilized. After three years of decline, we stopped bleeding students to Horizon Academy. Some families came back. Families considering leaving stayed. And we started attracting students who wanted something different—a school that offered technology and creativity, academics and hands-on learning.

We distinguished ourselves. We weren't the tech school. We were the school that embraced the full student experience. Parents started saying, "Montera is where my kid can build a chair in woodshop, play an instrument, and still be challenged academically."

Other schools took notice. Within five years, other middle schools in the district moved to block schedules. The model worked, and it spread.

The superintendent's investment paid off. The IB training elevated our teaching. Teachers weren't just delivering lessons—they were designing inquiry-based units that pushed students to think critically and creatively.

But the deeper result was this: we didn't try to become Horizon Academy. We became more ourselves.

Strategic Takeaways for Leaders

Know yourself before you know the competition. I couldn't build a strategy until I understood what Montera had that Horizon Academy didn't. We had space. We had tradition. We had the capacity to offer hands-on, experiential learning. Once I knew our strengths, I could build a plan around them.

Don't compete on your enemy's terms. Horizon Academy's identity was technology. If I'd tried to out-tech them, I would have lost. Instead, I differentiated. The strategic leader doesn't imitate the competition—they find the battlefield where they have the advantage.

Multi-year plans beat reactive fixes. Strategic change requires patience. A three-year plan gave us time to train teachers, build buy-in, and create sustainable systems. Quick fixes fail. Long-term strategies succeed.

Secure allies before you need them. The superintendent's support was critical. Without his willingness to fund IB training and new hires, the plan wouldn't have worked. I secured his buy-in in Year 1, before I needed the resources.

Involve your people in building the plan. I didn't impose the block schedule on teachers. I brought them into the design process. When people feel ownership, they commit. When they feel mandated, they resist.

The Deeper Lesson

Sun Tzu wrote, "The general who wins a battle makes many calculations in his temple before the battle is fought."

The "temple" isn't a physical place. It's the space where you think, plan, and prepare before you act. For me, the temple was my office after hours—data on the table, asking hard questions before I moved:

What are we really fighting?

What do we have that others don't?

What battle can we actually win?

At Montera, I spent a year in the temple. I studied Horizon Academy. I studied us. I built a three-year plan. I secured allies. I involved my staff.

And by the time we launched, the battle was already half-won.

Too many school leaders skip the temple. They see a problem and react immediately. They implement the first solution that sounds good. They copy what another school is doing without asking whether it fits their context.

And they lose.

Strategic leadership isn't about moving fast. It's about moving smart. It's about doing the hard work of planning when there's no visible progress to celebrate.

Horizon Academy was never our enemy. They were our competition. And instead of trying to beat them at their game, we played ours.

That's the art of laying plans.

Reflection Questions

Are you reacting to problems as they arise, or building multi-year strategies to address systemic challenges?

Do you know your competition well enough to understand what they offer that you don't—and what you offer that they can't?

When was the last time you spent serious time "in the temple"—thinking, planning, and preparing before acting?

Attack by Stratagem
Building Influence and Allies

The Wisdom of Sun Tzu

"Supreme excellence consists in breaking the enemy's resistance without fighting."

Interpretation: Winning Through Relationship, Not Confrontation

Sun Tzu understood something that takes most leaders years to learn: force is expensive, slow, and often counterproductive. The general who has to fight every battle has already lost the war of strategy.

In school leadership, this wisdom is equally true. You don't have the luxury of commanding compliance. You can't order teachers to be passionate or parents to be supportive. The principal who relies on positional authority—"because I said so"—will find themselves fighting exhausting battles on every front.

The master strategist wins before the conflict begins. They shape the conditions, build alliances, and create situations where the "enemy" becomes irrelevant or, better yet, becomes an ally.

When I transitioned from military service to education, I brought with me an understanding of command presence and decisive action. What I had to unlearn was the impulse to meet resistance with force. In the military, a lawful order is a lawful order. In schools? Every decision is a negotiation. Every change initiative is a sales pitch. Every conflict is an opportunity to either build trust or burn it down.

The principals who thrive are those who master the art of influence without intimidation, persuasion without politics, and leadership without leaving bodies in their wake.

Real-World Example: The Union Rep Who Tested Every Boundary

Let me tell you about Rita.

Rita had spent nearly three decades in the classroom as a 6th-grade math and science teacher. Everyone in the district knew her name.

Rita was the building union representative. But more than that, she was the union's proxy on campus—and in my district, the union was powerful, organized, and constantly probing for leverage. Every new principal was a test case: How far could they be pushed? What would they fight for? Where were they weak?

Rita wasn't personally hostile. She was professional, even cordial in our first meeting. But I could see the calculation in her eyes. She was taking my measure, figuring out what kind of leader I'd be.

Our district had a history. The previous principal had been a fighter—constantly battling the union, drawing lines in the sand, treating every disagreement as a war to be won. Staff morale was terrible. The union had grown defensive, adversarial, and dug in.

The problem was that previous leadership had trained the union to expect a fight.

I understood the game. When you're new to command, people test you to see if you have a backbone. The question wasn't whether Rita and I would clash. The question was whether I'd meet that test with confrontation or strategy.

I chose strategy. But first, I did reconnaissance.

Over the next two weeks, I learned everything I could about Rita:

Students loved her classes—she once ate bugs herself as part of a hands-on science lesson challenge

She mentored every new math and science teacher, often on her own time

Her classroom was immaculate, her lessons rigorous, her expectations sky-high

Students feared her, but alumni came back to thank her

Most importantly, I learned this: Rita wasn't the problem. She was doing exactly what a good union rep should do—advocate for her members and protect teachers from arbitrary decisions.

The problem was that previous leadership had trained the union to expect weakness or combat. Every interaction had been adversarial. Every pushback had ended in grievances and grudges.

Rita didn't need to see me as an enemy. She just needed to see me as someone who could be moved. My job was to change that calculation—not through confrontation, but through respect, consistency, and strategic partnership.

The Stratagem: Build the Alliance Before You Need It

I didn't wait for the first conflict. I went to Rita's classroom after school during my second week.

"Rita, I need to understand how things work here. You've been in this building longer than anyone. I'd like to meet with you weekly—not as adversaries, but as partners. You tell me what teachers need. I'll tell you what I'm thinking. We hash it out before it becomes a problem."

She was skeptical. "The last principal said something similar. Then he'd make decisions without telling me, and I'd hear about it from angry teachers."

"Then let's set a ground rule: no surprises. If I'm planning something that affects your members, you hear it from me first. And if you've got concerns brewing, I hear them from you before they become grievances."

"And if we disagree?"

"Then we disagree like professionals. You make your case. I make mine. Sometimes you'll convince me. Sometimes I'll hold my ground. But you'll always know I listened and considered your perspective."

She studied me for a long moment. "Okay. Let's try it."

We met every Wednesday morning at 7:30 AM. Coffee, no agenda, just honest conversation. In those meetings, I learned what mattered to teachers. She learned what I was willing to fight for and what was negotiable.

The Weekly Meetings: Where Strategy Happened

Those meetings became the most valuable hour of my week. Rita would bring concerns—sometimes legitimate, sometimes union posturing. I learned to tell the difference.

When she fought for planning time or reasonable class sizes, I backed her completely. When she pushed back on accountability measures that were non-negotiable, I held firm—but I explained my reasoning and asked for her input on implementation.

Sometimes she won. When I wanted to change the bell schedule, she made a compelling case that the impact on working parents hadn't been considered. I adjusted the plan. She saw that I could be moved by good arguments, not just pressure.

Most times, I held my ground. But even when I didn't change course, Rita knew she'd been heard. That respect mattered more than winning every battle.

The union still filed grievances occasionally—that was their job. But Rita would call me first: "Hey, this is coming. Here's why. Let's see if we can solve it before it goes formal."

Half the time, we did.

The Turning Point: When the Alliance Was Tested

Twelve weeks into the school year, we had a crisis. A first-year teacher on a temporary contract was failing—classroom management in shambles, parents flooding my inbox, students learning nothing.

Because Rita and I had been meeting weekly, she already knew about the situation. I'd brought it to her early: "I've got a teacher who's drowning. Here's what I'm seeing. What can we do to support her?"

We tried everything. Rita connected her with a mentor teacher. I reduced her extracurricular duties. We provided professional development on classroom management. I observed weekly and gave specific feedback. Rita checked in regularly, offering support and resources.

Nothing changed. If anything, things got worse.

In our Wednesday morning meeting, I laid it out honestly: "Rita, we've tried. You've seen me try. I can't let this go on through the end of the year. These kids deserve better."

She was quiet for a moment. Then: "What are you thinking?"

"She's on a temporary contract. I'm thinking we make a decision at winter break. If there's no significant improvement by then, we let her go. But I want to give her every chance to turn it around, and I need you to agree that we've done everything we could."

Rita nodded slowly. "Okay. But here's the deal: We document everything. Every support we provide, every conversation, every observation. If this goes sideways, I need to show my members that you did this right."

"Agreed. And Rita—I'm not trying to fire my way to success. I'm trying to save a teacher if we can. But if we can't, I need to protect those students."

"I know. That's why I'm saying yes."

We worked together over the next month. Rita continued mentoring. I continued observing and coaching. The teacher showed effort, but not improvement. By December, it was clear.

I met with the teacher and explained that she would be released. It was a hard conversation, but not a surprising one—she'd known all along where things stood.

Rita was there for the follow-up meeting with me afterward. "You did right by her," she said. "And more importantly, you did right by those kids."

The Outcome

Rita never became my best friend. We remained in our respective roles—principal and union representative, often on opposite sides of the table. But we operated with mutual respect.

She knew I wouldn't roll over just to avoid conflict. I knew she'd fight hard for her people, but she'd fight fair.

When I needed to push a difficult initiative, she'd tell me privately where the resistance would come from and how to frame it. When I made mistakes, she'd tell me directly instead of filing a grievance. When the district tried to force a curriculum program I knew was wrong for our students, Rita stood with me in opposition—even though it put her at odds with district union leadership.

The day I left that school for a new assignment, Rita came to my office. She handed me a card.

Inside, she'd written: "You earned this. Great working with you."

I still have that card.

Strategic Takeaways for Leaders

Resistance is often organizational, not personal. Union representatives aren't your enemies—they're doing their job. The adversarial dynamic often comes from past leadership failures, not present personalities. Understand the history that created the tension.

Build alliances before you need them. Don't wait for conflict to start building relationships. Regular, honest communication with key influencers creates partnership before problems arise. The alliance you build in peace will serve you in crisis.

Listening doesn't mean surrendering. You can hear someone's perspective fully, consider it genuinely, and still hold your ground. When people know you'll truly listen before deciding, they accept your decisions more readily, even when they disagree.

Consistency builds credibility. The union rep who meets with you weekly learns what you stand for and what you'll bend on. When people can predict your reasoning, they stop testing you and start working with you.

Partnership doesn't mean agreement. You will have non-negotiables. So will the union. Rita and I didn't agree on everything. But we agreed to respect the process and each other's roles.

The Deeper Lesson

In the military, I learned that the most respected leaders weren't the loudest or the most aggressive—they were the ones who took care of their people. They fought for their troops, listened when it mattered, and earned loyalty through action, not rank.

School leadership is no different. You don't win by asserting dominance. You win by building a coalition of people who trust that you see them, value them, and will fight for what's right even when it's hard.

Rita didn't become my ally because I defeated her. She became my ally because I refused to treat her as an enemy.

That's the supreme art of leadership: to transform opposition into partnership, not through manipulation or charm, but through genuine respect and consistent action.

Sun Tzu was right. The best generals don't fight battles. They make battles unnecessary.

Reflection Questions

Who in your building sees you as "the enemy"? What conditions created that perception?

What would change if you sought to understand their story before trying to change their mind?

Who are your Ritas—the skeptics whose conversion would shift the entire culture?

Energy (Morale and Momentum)

Harnessing Staff Energy Through Purpose and Clarity

The Wisdom of Sun Tzu

"Energy may be likened to the bending of a crossbow; decision, to the releasing of a trigger."

"The control of a large force is the same principle as the control of a few men: it is merely a question of instituting signs and signals."

═══════════════════

Interpretation: The Leader's Calculus of Energy

Sun Tzu understood something modern leadership books often miss: morale isn't about motivation speeches or pizza parties. It's about the efficient management of collective energy—knowing when to bend the bow, when to release the arrow, and critically, when to let the bow rest before it breaks.

In schools, those "signals" Sun Tzu mentioned are your calendar, your meeting rhythms, what you choose to protect and what you're willing to cancel. Those choices tell people whether their energy matters.

A fighting force—whether it's a Marine rifle company or a middle school teaching staff—has a finite reserve of energy. Push too hard for too long, and you don't get maximum effort. You get collapse.

In my years leading Marines, I learned that troop morale isn't measured by how loud they cheer at a pep rally. It's measured by whether they trust you enough to follow you into the difficult moments. That trust is built through one consistent principle: leaders who take care of their people get more from their people—not through coercion, but through loyalty.

I carried that lesson into education. And nowhere was it tested more than during the pandemic.

Real-World Example: The Staff Meeting That Turned the Tide

It was October 2020. Three months into full remote learning. Three months of Schoology assignments, Zoom fatigue, and the slow erosion of every system we'd built for connection and culture.

My staff was drowning.

Every Wednesday, our district held minimum days for professional development. Staff would finish their online classes, then immediately log into a Zoom meeting for PD. It wasn't working. Cameras off. Silent chats. Even my strongest teachers—the ones who usually carried the energy—looked hollowed out.

I knew what I was seeing because I'd seen it before. In the military, we called it "the thousand-yard stare." It's what happens when people are asked to operate at maximum capacity with no relief in sight. They're not defiant. They're not lazy. They're simply out of fuel.

That same week, we had our monthly principals' meeting with the superintendent. The message was clear: morale is dropping across the district. Teachers are struggling. We need to refocus.

Your assignment: conduct a PD session next Wednesday on classroom management and student discipline in the virtual environment.

I hung up from that Zoom and stared at my screen.

Discipline? Classroom management strategies? We were going to ask teachers—who were juggling their own children's remote learning, caring for sick family members, and teaching from their kitchen tables—to sit through a PowerPoint on consequences and accountability?

No.

I thought about what my battalion commander once told me during a particularly brutal training cycle: "If you take care of your Marines, your Marines will take care of you."

My staff didn't need another strategy session. They needed permission to breathe.

The Decision: Contextual Judgment

That Wednesday, I logged into our staff Zoom meeting at 1:00 PM. Fifty little rectangles appeared on my screen—some with cameras on, most off. Those who were visible looked tired. A few were clearly still finishing lunch. One teacher was visibly multitasking with her own child climbing on her lap.

I didn't share my screen. I didn't launch a presentation. I didn't even have an agenda slide prepared.

I wasn't being reckless. I knew my superintendent, I knew our relationship, and I was prepared to own the decision if it backfired. But I also knew my people—and what they needed wasn't another strategy session.

I just talked.

"Good afternoon, everyone. I know we were supposed to do PD on classroom management today. I'm not doing that. Here's why: I don't think you need another training right now. I think you need a break. So here's today's professional development—self-care.

Log off this call. Go do something you enjoy. Take a walk. Take a nap. Play with your kids. Watch Netflix. Binge-eat Halloween candy. I don't care what you do, as long as it has nothing to do with school.

I'll see you tomorrow. Take care of yourselves."

There was a long pause. A few cameras flickered on—confused faces, like they were waiting for the punchline.

Then the chat exploded.

"Are you serious?"

"Wait—we can really just log off?"

"Thank you."

"THANK YOU."

"You have no idea how much I needed this."

I smiled. "I'm serious. Go. I'll handle any questions from the district. This is on me."

Within thirty seconds, the Zoom room was empty. Just me and a blank screen.

I sat there for a moment, hoping I'd made the right call. Then I logged off and went for a run.

The Fallback: Admitting What You Did and Why

Two weeks later, we had another principals' meeting. The superintendent opened with a question: "I want to hear what you all are doing to support staff morale. Some of you have been really creative. Let's share out."

Several principals talked about wellness newsletters, shout-outs in staff meetings, and "teacher appreciation" initiatives—digital gift cards, coffee deliveries, things like that. All good ideas. All surface-level.

Then the superintendent called on me. "What about you? What are you doing?"

I took a breath. Here we go.

"I'm giving them time back. On our last PD day, I cancelled the planned training and told staff to log off and take care of themselves. No assignments. No expectations. Just rest."

The Zoom went quiet. I could see a few principals' reactions in their camera boxes—some nodding, others looking surprised.

The superintendent's voice cut through: "You didn't do the district PD?"

"No, ma'am. I didn't. And I'll do it again if my staff needs it."

Another pause. Then she smiled.

"Good. That's exactly what they needed. If you're not taking care of your people, nothing else matters. Keep doing that."

I exhaled.

She continued, "In fact, I want all of you to think about that. We can have the best curriculum, the best data systems, the best initiatives in the world. But if our people are broken, none of it works. Leadership right now isn't about compliance. It's about sustainability."

That comment gave me permission to make self-care PD a regular practice. Once a month, I'd cancel our planned session and give staff time back. No strings attached. No make-up work. Just rest.

The Impact: What Happened Next

The effects were immediate and sustained.

Morale shifted. Teachers started showing up to other meetings with more energy. Cameras came back on. Participation increased. The vibe in our Zoom rooms changed from resentful compliance to something closer to collaboration.

Trust deepened. Teachers started coming to me with real problems instead of hiding struggles. They knew I'd prioritize their humanity over bureaucratic appearances. One teacher told me, "You're the first principal who's ever treated us like we have lives outside this building."

I learned something critical. After that first self-care PD, several teachers thanked me privately. One said, "I used that time to help my daughter with her school assignments. She's in second grade and was melting down trying to navigate remote learning. I've been so stressed because I can't be there for her during the school day."

That's when it hit me: the same challenges our students were facing, our teachers were facing at home. Everyone was in lockdown. Everyone was trying to make remote learning work. My teachers weren't just educators during the pandemic—they were parents, caregivers, and humans trying to survive.

If I expected them to show up for our students, I had to make space for them to show up for their own families first.

The culture changed. By normalizing rest, I signaled that sustainability mattered more than performance theater. I wasn't interested in staff who looked busy on Zoom while quietly falling apart. I wanted a team that could go the distance—and that required protecting their energy, not extracting it.

Strategic Takeaways for Leaders

Recognize the signs of depleted energy before it's too late. Burnout doesn't announce itself with a resignation letter. It shows up as disengagement, cynicism, and exhaustion. Learn to read the room—or the Zoom.

Energy is finite. Manage it like a resource. You can't run your staff at 100% capacity indefinitely. Sun Tzu compared energy to a bent crossbow—hold it too long, and it loses tension. You have to release the pressure periodically or risk breaking the mechanism altogether.

Sometimes the best leadership decision is to do nothing. The instinct in a crisis is to do more—more initiatives, more training, more communication. But sometimes, the most strategic move is to stop. To give people permission to rest.

Your people will remember how you treated them in the hard times. That self-care PD became a story my teachers told for years—not because it was a grand gesture, but because it was the moment they felt someone finally had their back.

Protect your people by exercising strategic judgment. Sometimes leadership requires making difficult calls when prescribed solutions don't match your situation. That day, my staff needed rest more than another PD session—and the superintendent agreed.

The Deeper Lesson

Sun Tzu wrote, "He will win who knows when to fight and when not to fight."

That wisdom applies to more than battlefield tactics. It applies to how we lead people through exhaustion, crisis, and uncertainty. There are moments when you need to rally the troops, push hard, and demand excellence. And there are moments when the most courageous thing you can do is say, "Stop. Rest. We'll fight tomorrow."

The pandemic tested every leader's ability to distinguish between those moments. The principals who survived—and whose staff survived—weren't the ones who pushed harder. They were the ones who knew when to release the tension on the bow.

I learned in the Marine Corps that the strongest units aren't the ones that never get tired. They're the ones whose leaders understand fatigue, plan for recovery, and protect their people's capacity to keep going when it matters most.

That battalion commander was right: If you take care of your Marines, your Marines will take care of you.

The same is true in schools. If you take care of your teachers, they will take care of your students. But if you run them into the ground in the name of compliance, data, or district mandates, you'll end up with a staff that's physically present but emotionally gone.

Energy isn't something you demand. It's something you steward.

And sometimes, the best way to steward it is to give people permission to rest.

Reflection Questions

What are the signs of burnout in your building right now? Are people disengaging, going through the motions, showing up but not really present?

When was the last time you gave your staff permission to rest—with no strings attached? Not a "wellness activity" that's really more work. Actual rest.

Are you modeling sustainability, or are you modeling martyrdom? If you never rest, your staff will assume rest is weakness.

Building Adaptive Systems

Creating Structures That Function Under Pressure

The Wisdom of Sun Tzu

"The good fighters of old first put themselves beyond the possibility of defeat, and then waited for an opportunity of defeating the enemy."

Interpretation: Build Systems That Bend Without Breaking

Sun Tzu understood that victory comes from preparation, not reaction. The skilled general builds fortifications before the enemy arrives and creates conditions where defeat becomes nearly impossible.

But here's the critical insight: the best systems aren't rigid—they're adaptive.

In the military, we learned that no plan survives first contact. The commanders who thrived weren't the ones with the perfect plan—they were the ones whose systems could adjust mid-battle without collapsing.

School leadership demands the same flexibility. You need structures strong enough to function when you're not in the room, but flexible enough to adapt when circumstances change.

At Kaiser Elementary, I built a system using unconventional resources—and then watched it prove sustainable in ways I never anticipated.

Real-World Example: The Reading Crisis and the Unexpected Solution

When I arrived at Kaiser Elementary, the data told a nuanced story: while most students scored well, we had some students falling through the cracks—reading below grade level but not far enough behind to qualify for formal intervention

We needed a systematic way to identify these students early and provide consistent support. And we didn't have it.

No reading specialist. No interventionist. No funding.

I needed to build something with resources I didn't officially have.

The Discovery: A Conversation at Open House

A few weeks into the school year, we held an open house. I was greeting parents when one conversation changed everything.

A parent mentioned his wife. "She used to be a special education teacher. Stopped working when our kids were born. Now that our daughter's at Kaiser, she's thinking about getting back into it somehow."

My mind started calculating. "She was a special education teacher?"

"Yeah. Credentialed, experienced with reading interventions, the whole thing."

"Would she be interested in working part-time? Here? With students who need reading support?"

Two days later, I met Mrs. Bennett (pseudonym). Excellent teacher. Not looking for full-time work, but part-time at her daughter's school? Perfect.

Building the System: Response to Intervention

I proposed a Response to Intervention model—a tiered system designed to identify students early and provide targeted interventions before they fell too far behind.

Mrs. Bennett would be our Tier 2 intervention. Students who weren't progressing in regular instruction would get additional support—one-on-one interventions tailored to their specific needs.

The problem: I didn't have budget for this position.

The solution: I went to the PTA.

The Pitch: Data, Need, and Partnership

I scheduled a meeting with PTA leadership and came prepared.

I showed them the data: percentage of students reading below grade level, the achievement gap, the trajectory if we didn't intervene.

Then I explained the solution: hire a part-time Reading Interventionist. One-on-one support. Evidence-based strategies. Progress monitoring.

And I introduced Mrs. Bennett—credentialed, experienced, passionate.

"The district doesn't have funding for this position," I told them. "But you do. If the PTA can fund a part-time salary, we can build a system that changes trajectories for these kids."

They asked questions. How will you identify students? How will you measure progress? How long will students be in the program?

I had answers. Standardized test data for identification. Progress monitoring every two weeks. Students receive support until they reach grade-level benchmarks.

The PTA voted to fund it.

Implementing the System

Mrs. Bennett became our part-time Reading Interventionist. Here's how we structured it:

Identification: Standardized test data identified students reading significantly below grade level.

Pull-out model: Mrs. Bennett worked one-on-one during non-core instructional time—independent work periods, not direct instruction.

Evidence-based interventions: Research-backed reading strategies tailored to each student's specific needs—phonics, fluency, comprehension.

Progress monitoring: Every two weeks, she assessed progress and adjusted interventions. If a student wasn't responding, we changed the approach.

Teacher collaboration: Mrs. Bennett met regularly with classroom teachers to align her interventions with classroom instruction.

Exit criteria: When students reached grade-level benchmarks, they exited the program. Spots opened for new students.

The Results

Within one semester, reading levels started climbing. Students who'd been stuck below grade level for years were making measurable progress.

Teachers saw the difference. Parents saw it. And critically, the students saw it—they went from feeling "dumb" to feeling capable.

But the deeper victory was this: we'd built a sustainable system using unconventional resources.

When Systems Must Sustain: The Funding Question

The RTI system worked beautifully. Then we hit our first major test.

The PTA had funded the position, but they'd funded Mrs. Bennett specifically—someone they knew, whose daughter attended the school, who had deep ties to the community. Each year, we had to make the case again for continued funding.

Year one was easy. The results were immediate and visible. The PTA renewed without hesitation.

But year two required something different. We needed to show this wasn't just about Mrs. Bennett's talent—it was about a proven system that would continue delivering results.

I met with PTA leadership at their annual planning meeting. "Here's what we've accomplished." I showed them the data: reading growth, student success stories, teacher feedback.

"This system works. But it only works if we continue it. We've documented everything—the protocols, the interventions, the progress monitoring. This isn't dependent on any single person anymore. It's a structure."

They asked the right questions. How many students have you served? What's the success rate? Are classroom teachers supporting this, or just tolerating it?

I had answers. Over two years, we'd served 47 students. 82% reached grade-level benchmarks. Classroom teachers weren't just supporting it—they were requesting spots for their students.

The PTA didn't just vote to continue funding. They increased it.

And then they did something I hadn't expected: they raised the money at the annual school auction, making RTI funding a community-supported initiative. Parents bid on auction items knowing the proceeds would directly support reading intervention.

The system had moved beyond my office and beyond the PTA board room. It had become part of the school's identity.

Adapting the System: From Individual to Sustainable Structure

That community buy-in taught me something critical: systems built around individual talent are fragile. Systems built around documented process are sustainable.

Mrs. Bennett was exceptional. But if the system only worked because of her, then it wasn't really a system—it was just Mrs. Bennett.

So we made adjustments:

We created detailed protocols. Every intervention was documented. Progress monitoring tools were standardized. If Mrs. Bennett was absent, a substitute could step in without students missing sessions.

We expanded teacher training. Classroom teachers needed to know how to identify struggling readers early and how to support students between intervention sessions.

We built in redundancy. Backup materials. Alternative schedules. Clear communication pathways between Mrs. Bennett and classroom teachers.

The system became less dependent on any single person—including me.

What Happened After I Left

Three years after I left Kaiser, I ran into the new principal. "Is the RTI program still running?" I asked.

"Absolutely. I love it. Parents do too."

That's when I thought we'd built something that would last.

But I was wrong. When he left, the program stopped.

Here's what Sun Tzu understood that I had to learn the hard way: The leader who advances without seeking glory and retreats without shame—whose only concern is protecting their people—that's the leader worth following.

I built a system that worked. But I didn't build it to survive leaders who didn't share the strategic vision.

The program succeeded for a specific reason—it aligned resources with mission, used evidence to guide decisions, and engaged the community. But when new leadership arrived without understanding why those structures mattered, they dismantled what they didn't build.

That's the difference between a system and a sustainable system. A system works when the right people run it. A sustainable system works despite leadership changes because it's embedded in the culture, documented in practice, and owned by the community.

Here's what I should have done differently: trained more people in the thinking behind the system, not just the operations. Made the strategic logic visible. Created broader ownership beyond a few key players.

Because as every military leader learns: Strategy without tactics is the slowest route to victory. Tactics without strategy is the noise before defeat.

We had the tactics down perfectly. I just didn't make the strategy visible.

Strategic Takeaways for Leaders

Build systems using the resources you have, not the ones you wish you had. Strategic leaders don't wait for perfect resources—they creatively deploy what's available. The question isn't "What does the district provide?" It's "What can I access?"

Systems must be sustainable beyond your tenure—and that requires more than documentation. The RTI program survived one leadership transition because the new principal understood its value.

But when he left, it died. I had documented the protocols. I had secured the funding. But I hadn't embedded the strategic thinking that made those structures matter. The best systems don't just function when you're not in the room—they survive leaders who didn't build them

Pitch solutions with data, not appeals to emotion. The PTA didn't fund RTI because I asked nicely. They funded it because I showed them the data—the achievement gap, the trajectory, the measurable impact. Data creates urgency. Stories create buy-in. Use both.

Document the why, not just the what. When Mrs. Bennett eventually retired, the system survived because the new principal understood why it mattered, not just how it worked. Protocols matter. But strategic logic matters more. If your successor can't explain why the system exists, they won't fight to keep it.

Test your systems against the question: Will this work without me? If the answer is no, you haven't built a system—you've built a dependency. But ask the harder question too: Will this survive a leader who doesn't understand why it matters? That's the real test of sustainability.

The Deeper Lesson

In the Marine Corps, we learned that the best defensive positions weren't the most fortified—they were the most adaptable. A bunker that couldn't adjust to changing enemy movements became a tomb. A flexible defense that could reposition under fire survived.

School systems work the same way.

You need structures strong enough to function under normal conditions—schedules, protocols, intervention systems, accountability
measures. But you also need the wisdom to make those structures
transferable across leadership changes.

The RTI program at Kaiser worked because it was sustainable, evidence-based, and didn't require my constant oversight. It survived one
leadership transition because the new principal understood its value.
But when he left, it died.

I built a system that could bend under pressure—adjusting interventions when students didn't respond, transitioning to new staff.
But I didn't build a system that could survive a leader who didn't
understand why those structures mattered.

Sun Tzu wrote: *"The good fighters of old first put themselves
beyond the possibility of defeat."*

You put yourself beyond defeat by building systems before you need
them. But true sustainability means embedding the strategic logic so
deeply that future leaders can't dismantle what they don't understand—because they do understand it.

Strategic leaders don't just react to problems. They build structures
that prevent problems. And they make the thinking behind those
structures as visible as the structures themselves.

That's the lesson I learned too late. That's how you build something
that actually lasts..

Reflection Questions

What problem in your school keeps recurring because you don't have a system to address it?

What resources exist around you that you haven't leveraged? Parents? Community partners? Unconventional funding sources?

Will your best systems survive without you? If you left tomorrow, would your interventions, protocols, and structures continue—or would they collapse?

Knowing Your Terrain

Understanding Your School Before You Try to Change It

The Wisdom of Sun Tzu

"He who knows when he can fight and when he cannot will be victorious."

Interpretation: Context Is Everything

Sun Tzu devoted entire chapters to understanding terrain and situation because he knew: the same tactic that wins on one battlefield fails on another.

The general who doesn't study the ground—the hills, rivers, forests, and weather—walks into ambushes. The general who doesn't understand the situation—whether forces are desperate, surrounded, or on favorable ground—makes catastrophic mistakes.

School leadership is no different.

You cannot lead a school you don't understand. And understanding means more than reading test scores or walking the halls once. It means studying the culture, history, politics, relationships, and invisible dynamics that shape how people respond to you.

Every school has terrain:

The culture: unwritten rules, power dynamics, what's celebrated, what's avoided

The history: who came before you, what they did, what wounds they left

The stakeholders: who has influence, who resists, who's waiting to see what you'll do

The situation: are you walking into crisis, stability, or something in between?

Strategic leaders study this terrain before they act. Reactive leaders charge in with solutions and wonder why they fail.

At Kaiser Elementary, I walked into a school where the terrain was hostile—not because the people were bad, but because leadership had broken their trust. I had to understand that terrain before I could change it.

Real-World Example: Kaiser Elementary—When Trust Is the Terrain

When I was offered the principalship at Kaiser Elementary, I knew almost nothing about the school.

Kaiser sat in the Oakland Hills. Test scores were solid. The teachers were experienced, credentialed, deeply knowledgeable. On paper, it looked like a great school.

But something was broken.

Staff morale was shattered. Teachers were demoralized after years under a previous principal who'd lost their trust. Teachers who should have been thriving were just surviving. Talent was being wasted.

And I walked in as the outsider. New to elementary education. New to the community. No credibility. No relationships. A staff that had every reason to be skeptical of yet another new principal making promises.

For the first time in my career, I felt truly out of my depth.

That's when I turned to Sun Tzu.

The First Lesson: Know the Ground

Sun Tzu wrote: "He who knows when he can fight and when he cannot will be victorious."

I couldn't change Kaiser until I understood it. So I spent my first month doing reconnaissance.

I observed without intervening. I sat in classrooms. Not to evaluate—just to watch. I wanted to see what excellent teaching looked like at Kaiser, what the rhythm of the school felt like, what students responded to. I didn't offer feedback. I didn't suggest changes. I just watched and learned.

I listened more than I talked. I scheduled one-on-one conversations with every teacher. Not formal meetings—coffee, lunch, after-school chats. I asked three questions: What's working well at Kaiser? What's not working? If you were principal, what would you change first?

I took notes. I didn't defend the previous administration. I didn't make promises. I just listened.

I studied the history. I asked veteran staff: What was Kaiser like five years ago? Ten years ago? What changed? What stayed the same?

The principal before my immediate predecessor had been strong—loved by staff, trusted by families. Teachers remembered when Kaiser leadership worked. But the most recent principal had destroyed that foundation. Decision-making became erratic. Promises weren't kept. Teachers felt ignored, then micromanaged, then abandoned.

That history mattered. Trust wasn't just low—it was shattered. Teachers had trusted before and been burned.

I identified the power structure. Every school has formal leaders (principal, AP, department chairs) and informal leaders (the veteran teacher everyone respects, the union rep, the parent who runs the PTA).

Formal leaders have titles. Informal leaders have influence.

At Kaiser, the informal leaders were:

Sarah: 20-year veteran, beloved by staff, skeptical of all administrators

Marcus: union steward, protective of teachers, suspicious of change

Linda: parent leader, deeply invested in the school, wary of outsiders

If I wanted to lead Kaiser, I needed their trust. Not their compliance—their partnership.

The Second Lesson: Understand the Situation

Sun Tzu taught that different circumstances demand different tactics. Desperate ground requires different leadership than stable ground.

Kaiser was desperate ground.

Morale was broken. Trust was gone. Teachers were burned out. And I was an unknown quantity—someone they had no reason to believe in.

Sun Tzu wrote: "In desperate ground, I would proclaim to my soldiers the hopelessness of saving their lives."

That sounds bleak. But the wisdom is this: in desperate situations, honesty builds trust faster than optimism.

So in my first staff meeting, I didn't give a motivational speech. I told the truth.

The First Staff Meeting: Honesty Over Inspiration

I stood in front of 10 teachers who didn't know me and had no reason to trust me.

I didn't pretend everything was fine. I didn't promise quick fixes. I said:

"I know morale is low. I know trust has been broken. I know you've heard promises from administrators before, and those promises didn't hold. I'm not going to ask you to trust me yet—I haven't earned that. But here's what I will do:

I will listen before I act. I will be honest, even when the truth is hard. I will fight for what you need, even when it's uncomfortable for me. And I will show up, consistently, every day, until you believe I'm here for the right reasons.

I don't expect you to trust me today. But I'm asking for the chance to earn it."

The room was silent.

I continued: "I'm not here to prove I'm smarter than you. I'm here to lead a school where you can do your best work. Some of you are skeptical. That's fair. Some of you are exhausted. I get it. I didn't take this job to climb a ladder. I took it because this school deserves better than what it's been getting."

No applause. No visible reaction. Just quiet assessment.

But I'd set the tone: I wasn't going to lie to them. I was going to earn their trust, one decision at a time.

The Strategy: Build Trust Through Consistency

Over the next six months, I followed a deliberate strategy:

I kept promises—even small ones. If I said I'd get back to someone by Friday, I did. If I promised to look into a concern, I followed up. Trust isn't built through grand gestures. It's built through reliability.

I made myself visible. I was in the hallways every morning. I ate lunch in the staff room. I attended grade-level meetings. Teachers needed to see that I wasn't distant or disconnected—I was present.

I protected teachers publicly. When a parent complained about a teacher's grading policy, I backed the teacher completely. I met with the parent, explained the policy, and made it clear: I trust my teachers' professional judgment.

Teachers noticed. Word spread. "He actually has our backs."

I admitted when I didn't know something. In a leadership team meeting, a teacher asked a question about elementary literacy frameworks. I didn't know the answer. I could have faked it. Instead, I said, "I don't know. I'm new to elementary. Teach me."

That vulnerability mattered. It signaled: I'm not here to pretend I'm an expert. I'm here to learn and lead.

I fought battles that mattered to teachers. The district wanted to implement a new assessment system that would add hours of work for teachers. I went to the superintendent with a solution: "My staff is already underwater. But if you give us a sub, we can pull students out for assessment instead of adding hours after school."

The district approved it. Teachers saw that I was willing to advocate for them and find workable solutions.

The Terrain Shifted

By the end of my first year, the terrain at Kaiser had changed.

Staff morale wasn't perfect, but it was improving. Teachers who'd been skeptical were cautiously optimistic. Informal leaders who'd been resistant were starting to partner with me.

Sarah stopped by my office one day. "You're different from the last one," she said. "You actually listen."

Marcus started calling me before filing grievances. "Let's talk this through before it goes formal."

Linda became an advocate. "He's the real deal," she told other parents.

The terrain hadn't been favorable when I arrived. But I didn't try to force change before I understood it. I studied the ground. I adapted to the situation. I built trust through consistency.

And once the terrain shifted, everything else became possible.

Strategic Takeaways for Leaders

You cannot lead a school you don't understand. Study the culture, history, and power dynamics before you make changes. Spend your first 30-60 days in reconnaissance mode. Observe. Listen. Learn.

Informal leaders matter more than org charts. Every school has people with influence who don't have titles. Identify them. Build relationships with them. If you can't win their trust, you'll struggle to lead effectively.

Trust is the terrain. If it's broken, rebuild it first. At Kaiser, I couldn't implement new programs or push change until I'd rebuilt trust. Trying to lead without trust is like fighting on swampy ground—everything you do sinks.

Different situations demand different leadership. At Kaiser, I was on desperate ground—morale broken, trust shattered. That required honesty and humility, not confidence and vision. Know what situation you're in, and lead accordingly.

Honesty builds trust faster than optimism. When morale is low and skepticism is high, don't pretend everything is fine. Acknowledge reality. Tell the truth. Staff respect leaders who are honest about challenges more than leaders who fake positivity.

The Deeper Lesson

Sun Tzu's wisdom on terrain and situation isn't just about geography—it's about context. The same decision that works in one school fails in another. The same leadership style that succeeds with one staff alienates another.

In the military, we learned that the best commanders weren't the ones who imposed their preferred tactics on every battlefield. They were the ones who adapted tactics to fit the terrain.

At Kaiser, the terrain was hostile. Trust was broken. Morale was low. If I'd walked in with bold initiatives and high expectations, I would have failed. The ground wouldn't have supported it.

Instead, I studied the terrain. I understood the situation. I adapted my approach. And once the ground shifted—once trust was rebuilt—everything else became possible. ·

Three years later, Kaiser Elementary was transformed. The talented teachers who'd been demoralized were thriving. Staff morale was strong. Parents trusted us.

But that transformation didn't start with new programs or initiatives. It started with understanding the terrain and adapting to it.

Sun Tzu devoted an entire chapter to terrain—to knowing the ground you fight on. He understood that victory requires understanding both the landscape and the conditions you're operating in.

He was right. You can't win battles on ground you don't understand.

Study your school. Understand its history, culture, and people. Adapt your leadership to fit the situation you're in, not the one you wish you had.

Because the terrain won't shift for you. You have to shift with it first.

Reflection Questions

How much time did you spend studying your school before trying to change it? Did you observe, listen, and learn—or did you charge in with solutions?

Who are the informal leaders in your building? Do you know who has influence beyond their title?

Is trust the terrain at your school, or something else? What's the cultural dynamic you need to understand before you can lead effectively?

When Good Plans Fail
Knowing When to Retreat and Regroup

The Wisdom of Sun Tzu

"He who knows when he can fight and when he cannot will be victorious."

"There are roads which must not be followed."

═══════════════════════

Interpretation: Not Every Battle Can Be Won

Sun Tzu's wisdom wasn't just about winning—it was about knowing which battles not to fight.

The greatest generals didn't win every engagement. They won wars by choosing battlefields carefully, recognizing when terrain was unfavorable, and retreating strategically when victory wasn't achievable.

In school leadership, this is the hardest lesson to learn. We're trained to persist, to push through resistance, to "never give up." But strategic leadership requires the humility to recognize when a plan—no matter how good it looks on paper—simply won't work in your context.

And it requires the courage to abandon that plan before it destroys your credibility.

I learned this lesson the hard way at Montera Middle School, when a vision I was deeply committed to ran headfirst into reality—and reality won.

Real-World Example: The Mandarin Program That Wasn't Meant to Be

In Chapter 1, I told you about Montera's transformation: the block schedule, the IB training, the arts and music expansion. What I didn't tell you was the part of that vision that failed.

When we designed the new schedule, I didn't just want electives. I wanted something bold, something that would set Montera apart from every other middle school in Oakland: dual foreign language instruction.

Students would choose between Spanish and Mandarin.

Spanish made sense—it was practical, widely spoken in our community, and we had qualified teachers. But Mandarin? That was the differentiator. That was the move that would make families say, "Montera is preparing students for a global economy."

I'd done the research. Mandarin was increasingly valuable in business and diplomacy. Few middle schools offered it. If we could pull this off, we'd be the only school in the district providing this opportunity.

I pitched it to the superintendent. He loved it.

I pitched it to staff. They were intrigued, if skeptical.

I started recruiting.

And that's when everything fell apart.

The First Problem: The Teacher We Found Couldn't Adjust

After an extensive search, we finally found a Mandarin teacher. She was qualified, credentialed, and spoke the language fluently. On paper, she was exactly what we needed.

But once she started, the problems became clear. She couldn't adjust to teaching in the United States—specifically, to teaching American middle school students.

The teaching style she brought from her training didn't translate. Her classroom management struggled with the energy and dynamics of our students. The cultural gap between her expectations and our students' needs was wider than any of us had anticipated.

We provided support. We paired her with a mentor teacher. We adjusted her schedule. But the fundamental challenge remained: she wasn't able to adapt to the context of an American public middle school.

It wasn't her fault. It wasn't our students' fault. It was a mismatch that we should have anticipated but didn't.

The Second Problem: Students Didn't Want It

The parents had concerns, but we could have worked through those with better communication and clearer rationale.

The bigger problem was the students themselves. They didn't want to take Mandarin.

When we surveyed students about their language preferences, the results were overwhelming: the vast majority chose Spanish. Some wanted Spanish because their families spoke it. Others chose it because their friends were taking it. A few were intimidated by Mandarin's reputation for difficulty.

But the pattern was clear: we were trying to build a program that our students actively didn't want.

We could have mandated it—forced students into Mandarin classes regardless of their preference. But that would have guaranteed resentment, disengagement, and failure.

A language program only works if students are motivated to learn. And our students had made their choice clear.

The Third Problem: It Wasn't Working

We tried to make it work. For an entire year, we persisted.

The Mandarin teacher struggled. Students were disengaged. The classes that should have been exciting and innovative felt forced and frustrating.

By the end of the first year, it was clear: this wasn't sustainable.

I could have tried another year. Found a different teacher. Adjusted the approach again. But I'd learned enough from the first year to know the fundamental problem: we were fighting against reality.

The teacher couldn't adjust to our context. The students didn't want the class. And no amount of tweaking or supporting was going to change those core issues.

Sun Tzu wrote: ***"There are roads which must not be followed."***

After one full year of trying, I finally admitted I was on one of those roads. And I needed to turn around.

The Decision: Strategic Retreat

I called a meeting with my assistant principals.

"We're not doing Mandarin," I said.

They looked relieved.

"We're going all-in on Spanish. Robust program. Multiple levels. Strong instruction. We make Spanish the best middle school language program in the district."

"What about the families who were expecting Mandarin?" one AP asked.

"I'll own it. I'll tell them we couldn't make it work, and rather than offer a weak program, we're building a strong one in Spanish. It's not what I promised, but it's what's best for students."

It felt like failure. Because it was.

But it was also strategic. I could have kept pushing—hired an un-qualified teacher, forced the program through, and watched it collapse mid-year. That would have been worse. That would have damaged credibility, wasted resources, and hurt students.

Better to retreat now, regroup, and build something sustainable.

The Communication: Owning the Failure

At the end of that first year, I sent an email to all families. I didn't hide behind excuses or blame the teacher. I was direct:

"After one year of implementing our dual-language program, we've made the decision to focus exclusively on Spanish moving forward. While we worked hard to make the Mandarin program successful, it became clear that we couldn't provide the quality of instruction our students deserve.

The challenge wasn't just about finding the right teacher—it was about student engagement, cultural fit, and building a program that truly serves our community's needs and interests.

Rather than continue with a program that isn't working, we're pivot-ing to build the strongest Spanish program in the district. Starting next year, we will offer a comprehensive three-year Spanish sequence—the only middle school in our district to do so.

I know we started this year with different expectations. But our commitment is to offer programs that are excellent, not just available.

This was my decision, and I take full responsibility for it."

The response was mixed. A few families were disappointed. Most understood. Some were relieved—they'd been nervous about Mandarin from the start.

And critically, staff saw that I was willing to admit when a plan wasn't working. That built trust.

The Pivot: Making Spanish Excellent

If Mandarin was off the table, Spanish had to be exceptional. Not just "good enough"—excellent.

We hired two additional Spanish teachers. We built a comprehensive three-year sequence (6th, 7th, 8th grade) that aligned with high school placement—making us the only middle school in the district to offer three full years of Spanish instruction. We integrated cultural components—food, music, literature—so it wasn't just grammar drills.

And it worked. Within two years, Montera's Spanish program was one of the strongest in the district. Students were entering high school Spanish II or III, ahead of their peers from other middle schools. Parents were proud. Teachers were engaged.

Students who completed all three years at Montera had a significant advantage when they reached high school. They could skip introductory classes and move directly into advanced Spanish courses, giving them a pathway to AP Spanish and beyond.

But more importantly, I'd learned a lesson that would serve me for the rest of my career: Vision without feasibility is fantasy.

Strategic Takeaways for Leaders

Not every battle can be won—know when to retreat. Sun Tzu's wisdom isn't just about winning. It's about recognizing when the terrain, the resources, or the timing make victory impossible. Strategic retreat saved credibility and resources for battles I could win.

Feasibility matters as much as vision. Mandarin was a great idea in theory. But theory doesn't teach classes. Having credentials isn't enough—you need the right fit for your specific environment. Before you commit to a bold initiative, ask: Can we actually execute this well?

Check your vision against community priorities—and student interest. I assumed students would embrace Mandarin as an exciting opportunity. Instead, they overwhelmingly chose Spanish. Strategic leaders don't just consider parent needs—they listen to the students themselves. A program can't succeed if students are forced into it against their will.

Admitting failure builds trust if you do it right. When I told families we weren't doing Mandarin, I didn't make excuses or blame others. I owned it. Leaders who hide mistakes lose credibility. Leaders who own them and course-correct earn respect.

Pivot with purpose, not panic. Abandoning Mandarin wasn't giving up—it was redirecting resources toward something sustainable.

The pivot to excellent Spanish instruction salvaged the initiative. When you retreat, make sure you're retreating toward something better, not just away from failure.

The Deeper Lesson

I wanted Mandarin to work because it was my idea. It was bold, innovative, differentiating. Letting it go felt like admitting I'd been wrong.

But strategic leadership isn't about being right. It's about doing what's best for students, even when it means abandoning a plan you were personally invested in.

The Mandarin program failed. But the lesson didn't.

Because of that failure, I learned to vet feasibility before committing, check community alignment before announcing, recognize the difference between persistence and stubbornness, and retreat strategically when the terrain is unfavorable.

And those lessons made me a better leader.

Sun Tzu was right: *"He who knows when he can fight and when he cannot will be victorious."*

I didn't fight for Mandarin. I pivoted to Spanish. And that pivot—grounded in reality, not ego—became one of the strongest programs at Montera.

Sometimes, the most strategic move is knowing when to walk away.

Reflection Questions

What initiative are you holding onto that the evidence says won't work? Are you persisting because it's achievable, or because you don't want to admit failure?

Have you checked your vision against community priorities? Or are you assuming families want what you think they should want?

Are you confusing persistence with stubbornness? Strategic leaders know the difference. Which one is driving your current decisions?

Maneuvering (Decision-Making and Adaptability)

Navigating Bureaucracy and Unexpected Crises

The Wisdom of Sun Tzu

"In all fighting, the direct method may be used for joining battle, but indirect methods will be needed in order to secure victory."

"Let your plans be dark and impenetrable as night, and when you move, fall like a thunderbolt."

Interpretation: The Art of the Tactical Pivot

Sun Tzu's genius wasn't in brute force—it was in maneuverability. The ability to change direction mid-battle, to see when the direct approach has failed, and to find an unexpected angle that renders the enemy's defenses irrelevant.

In war, the general who can only fight one way will eventually meet an obstacle they cannot overcome. The master strategist has multiple options, reads the terrain in real time, and adapts faster than the opponent can react.

School leadership demands the same agility. You will face moments where the "right" move—the one the handbook prescribes, the one you planned for, the one that should work—simply won't. The door won't open. The student won't comply. The system will fail. And in that moment, with everyone watching, you have a choice: dig in and escalate, or maneuver.

The leaders who survive aren't the ones with the best plans. They're the ones who can abandon the plan when the plan stops working.

In the military, we trained for contingencies. Every mission had a primary plan and at least two backup plans. But no plan survives first contact. The question isn't whether you'll have to adapt—it's whether you'll recognize the moment when adaptation is required and have the composure to execute it without hesitation.

Your job as a leader isn't to force compliance. It's to maneuver around resistance in a way that accomplishes the mission without leaving casualties in your wake.

Real-World Example: The Student Who Wouldn't Leave the Room

Her name was Jasmine. Seventh grader. Natural leader. When she spoke, people listened. She was a force—the kind of student you want on your side.

But on this particular day, she was testing me.

We'd scheduled a restorative justice circle to address a conflict between several girls. The situation had escalated over social media, spilled into the hallways, and was threatening to turn into a larger issue if we didn't intervene.

The circle was being held in our restorative justice coordinator's classroom. The girls directly involved were seated. The facilitator was ready. Everything was in place.

Then Jasmine walked in.

She wasn't part of the conflict. She hadn't been named by any of the students involved. But one of the girls was her friend, and Jasmine wasn't about to let her sit in that circle alone.

Our RJ coordinator approached her gently. "Jasmine, this circle is just for the students directly involved. I need you to step out."

Jasmine didn't move. "I'm staying."

The coordinator tried again, more firmly this time. "Jasmine, I appreciate you wanting to support your friend, but this process only works if we keep it to the people involved. Please leave."

"No."

Now it was a problem. The coordinator called security. Our school safety officer—someone Jasmine knew and generally respected—came in and made the same request.

"Jasmine, you need to leave the room."

She looked him in the eye. "I'm not going anywhere."

That's when they called me.

The Moment of Decision

I walked into the room and immediately felt the tension. Jasmine was seated near her friend, arms crossed, jaw set. The other students were watching. The adults—coordinator, security, a counselor who'd been pulled in—were all standing, waiting to see what I would do.

This was a test. Not just for Jasmine, but for me. Everyone in that room was asking the same silent question: Who's really in charge here, and how will he prove it?

I could feel the weight of expectations. The adults expected me to assert authority—to make it clear that defiance has consequences. The students expected me to escalate—to raise my voice, threaten consequences, maybe even call her parents or remove her by force.

But I knew Jasmine. I'd been watching her for months. This wasn't rebellion for rebellion's sake. This was loyalty. She believed her friend needed her, and she wasn't going to abandon her just because an adult said so.

I walked over and crouched down so I was at her eye level. Calm. No aggression. No performance.

"Jasmine, I need you to leave so we can hold this circle. Can you do that for me?"

She looked at me—not with anger, but with something closer to resolve. "No. I'm not leaving."

I straightened up and asked again, making sure she understood this was serious. "I'm asking you one more time. Will you step out?"

She didn't hesitate. "No."

The room was silent. Every eye was on me. This was the moment where most administrators would escalate. Write her up. Call her parents. Remove her forcibly if necessary. Make an example.

The direct method had clearly failed—she wasn't leaving. Sun Tzu would say the time for indirect methods had arrived.

I looked at Jasmine. Then at the coordinator. Then at the door.

And I maneuvered.

The Indirect Method

I turned to the restorative justice coordinator and held out my keys. "Take the circle to the conference room down the hall. I'll meet you there in a few minutes."

The coordinator blinked. "What?"

"Move the circle. She's not leaving. So we will."

For a second, no one moved. Then the coordinator took my keys. The students stood. The adults started guiding them out. One by one, they filed past Jasmine, who sat frozen in her chair, eyes wide.

Within sixty seconds, the room was empty. Just me and Jasmine.

She stared at me, stunned. "Wait. What just happened?"

I pulled up a chair and sat down across from her. "You said you weren't leaving. So I let you stay. But the circle still has to happen, and it's happening down the hall."

I paused. "You won. You stayed. But the circle still happened. Now we get to decide what that 'win' means."

She opened her mouth. Closed it. Then said, quietly, "I didn't think you'd do that."

"I know. The circle moved forward, you stayed, and now we're having a real conversation. Nobody lost."

The Real Conversation

We sat in silence for a moment. She was processing. I could see the defiance draining out of her, replaced by something else—confusion, maybe, or the realization that she'd just been outmaneuvered.

Finally, she said, "Are you going to suspend me?"

"Should I?"

"I... I don't know. I didn't do what you asked."

"You didn't. But I'm not interested in punishing you, Jasmine. I'm interested in understanding you. Why did you refuse to leave?"

She hesitated, then the words came out in a rush. "Because everyone always leaves her. Her mom's never around. Her friends drop her whenever there's drama. I knew she was scared to sit in that circle alone, and I wasn't going to let that happen."

I nodded. "So you were protecting her."

"Yeah."

"That's leadership, Jasmine."

She looked up, surprised.

"You saw someone who needed support, and you stepped up. That takes courage. But here's the thing—you wanted to help your friend, but the way you chose to do it disrupted the process that was actually designed to help her. You became the problem you were trying to solve."

She was quiet, absorbing that.

I continued. "I've watched you lead. Students listen to you. They follow you. That's rare, and it's powerful. But power without strategy is just chaos. You have influence—real influence. You can use it to build things or to break things. Today, you used it to break things."

She was leaning forward now, engaged. "So what should I have done?"

"You could have talked to me before the circle. You could have asked if there was a way for you to support your friend without disrupting the process. You could have waited outside the room and been there for her afterward. There were a dozen ways to show loyalty without defiance. But you picked the hardest one—the one that forced everyone to choose between you and the process."

She nodded slowly. "I didn't think about it like that."

"I know. But now you can. And here's what I want from you, Jasmine—I want you to use that leadership for something bigger. Not just for your friends. For the whole school. I need students like you who aren't afraid to step up. But I need you to step up with me, not against me."

Her eyes widened. "Like how?"

"We'll figure that out. But first, you need to understand something. When you walk out of this room, the other students are going to ask what happened. Some of them are going to think I punished you. Others are going to think you got away with something. What you tell them matters. Because if you say, 'He didn't do anything, I won,' you'll lose my trust. But if you say, 'We talked, and I learned something,' you'll gain my respect. And respect is worth more than winning."

She was quiet for a long moment. Then she said, "Can I go check on my friend when the circle is over?"

"Absolutely. That's exactly what a leader does."

The Outcome

Jasmine left that room different than she came in. Not broken. Not defeated. But redirected.

The restorative circle proceeded smoothly in the conference room. The girls talked, listened, and reached a resolution. No one left angry. No one left blamed. The process worked the way it was supposed to.

When it was over, Jasmine was waiting outside. She didn't interrupt. She didn't demand access. She just waited. And when her friend came out, she was there—not as a disruptor, but as a supporter.

Over the next few months, Jasmine became one of my most valuable allies. She helped mediate conflicts between students. She spoke at assemblies about peer leadership. She organized a student-led initiative to improve school culture. She didn't stop being strong-willed—but she learned to channel that strength strategically.

When she graduated eighth grade and moved on to high school, we stayed in touch. She became senior class president. She led student government. She used her influence to build things, not break them.

Months later, I ran into her mother at a community event. She laughed and said, "I don't know what you said to Jasmine that day, but you got her. She talks about you all the time."

I smiled. "I didn't get her. I just gave her a different battlefield."

Strategic Takeaways for Leaders

Recognize when the direct method has failed. When your first approach doesn't work—and your second doesn't either—stop repeating the same move. If the student won't leave, don't keep asking. Maneuver.

Adapt faster than the situation can escalate. The moment I realized Jasmine wasn't going to leave, I had a choice: escalate or pivot. Escalation would have "won" in the short term—but I would have lost her trust, alienated the other students, and turned a teachable moment into a power struggle. The pivot preserved the relationship and accomplished the mission.

Don't confuse winning the battle with winning the war. Getting Jasmine out of that room would have been a battle. Building her into a leader was the war. If I'd forced compliance, I would have won that day and lost everything that came after.

Use resistance as an opportunity, not a threat. Jasmine's defiance wasn't a problem to be solved—it was information to be used. She was telling me something important: she valued loyalty, she wasn't afraid to stand her ground, and she had influence. Those are leadership qualities.

Make the problem irrelevant instead of fighting it. The problem wasn't Jasmine. The problem was that Jasmine's presence was disrupting the circle. So instead of fighting Jasmine, I removed the circle. She got to stay, and we got to proceed. No casualties. No drama. Just tactical maneuverability.

The Deeper Lesson

Sun Tzu's principle of maneuverability isn't about being slippery or avoiding confrontation. It's about strategic flexibility—the ability to see multiple paths and choose the one that accomplishes the mission with the least cost.

In the Marine Corps, I learned that the best infantry officers weren't the ones who charged straight ahead. They were the ones who could read the terrain, anticipate the enemy's moves, and find the flanking route no one expected. They won not because they were stronger, but because they were smarter and faster.

School leadership is no different. You will face moments where the prescribed response—the one in the handbook, the one you planned for—simply won't work. The student won't comply. The parent won't listen. The system will fail you.

And in that moment, you have two choices: insist on the direct method and escalate into a battle you don't need to fight, or maneuver around the obstacle and accomplish your mission through an indirect path.

The leaders who thrive are the ones who can pivot without hesitation, adapt without panic, and find a third option when everyone else sees only two.

Jasmine taught me that day that the most powerful move isn't always the most forceful one. Sometimes, the most powerful move is the one nobody expects—the one that changes the battlefield entirely.

Moving the circle instead of Jasmine was that "thunderbolt"—sudden, unexpected, and decisive.

Sun Tzu was right: when you move, fall like a thunderbolt. But make sure you're striking the right target.

Reflection Questions

When was the last time you insisted on the direct method when an indirect approach would have worked better? Did you escalate a situation because you felt you had to "win," even though winning cost you something more valuable?

Who in your building is like Jasmine—defiant, strong-willed, but fundamentally a leader? Are you treating them as a problem to be managed, or as a force to be redirected?

What "battles" are you fighting right now that don't need to be fought? What would happen if you maneuvered around them instead of through them?

Leading Through Crisis

Preparation, Presence, and Information

The Wisdom of Sun Tzu

"The skillful leader cultivates the situation to his advantage before the crisis arrives."

Interpretation: Preparation Before Panic

Sun Tzu's teaching on desperate situations is often misunderstood. The focus falls on the dramatic moment—the fight, the siege, the last stand. But the real wisdom is here: "the skillful leader cultivates the situation to his advantage before the crisis arrives."

Crisis leadership isn't about heroic decisions under fire—it's the unglamorous preparation long before anyone knows a storm is coming: reading weak signals, building flexible systems, and creating trust before you need to spend it.

In military planning, we called this war-gaming—thinking through scenarios before they happened, pre-positioning resources, and establishing protocols so that when chaos hit, muscle memory took over. The leaders who thrived in crisis weren't the ones who made brilliant split-second decisions. They were the ones who had already made most of the decisions weeks or months earlier.

School leadership demands the same discipline. You will face crises—it's not a matter of if, but when. A student incident that goes viral. A staff member accused of misconduct. A natural disaster. A pandemic.

The question isn't whether you'll face desperate situations. The question is whether you'll be ready when they arrive.

Real-World Example: The Crisis No One Saw Coming

Let me take you back to late February 2020.

COVID-19 was in the news, but it still felt distant—something happening elsewhere, maybe overseas, but not here. Not yet. Schools were operating normally. Life was normal.

But I was uneasy.

My leadership team and I had started paying attention. Cases were increasing. The tone in the news was shifting from "concern" to "alarm." We began asking questions: What if schools close? What if this becomes serious? What are we even supposed to do?

We didn't have answers. But we were watching.

The Signal

Then one evening in early March, my wife came home from work. She's in the corporate world—finance, logistics, the kind of industry that moves fast and takes risk seriously.

"We're shutting down," she said. "The whole company. Everyone's going remote starting Monday."

I stared at her. "The whole company?"

"They're not waiting for government orders. Leadership said if we wait, it'll be too late to transition smoothly."

That night, I couldn't sleep. If the corporate world—with all its resources and contingency planning—was moving this decisively, what did that mean for schools? We didn't have their infrastructure or flexibility. And we had 700 kids who depended on us not just for education, but for meals, safety, and stability.

The next morning, I called an emergency meeting with my leadership team.

"I don't know if schools will close," I said. "But we're going to act like they will—starting now."

The Decision: Build the System Before You Need It

We had a choice to make, and we had to make it fast.

The district's plan—so far as there was one—was to use Zoom for instruction if schools closed. Teachers would hold live video classes. Simple, right?

But I saw problems with that approach:

Not all students had reliable internet or devices

Live classes required real-time participation—what about families with multiple kids sharing one device?

Zoom was fine for meetings, weak for structured curriculum

Teachers had no training in remote instruction

We needed something more robust. Something asynchronous. Something that gave structure and routine when everything else was falling apart.

We already used a platform called Schoology—a learning management system where teachers could post assignments, readings, and resources. Most used it lightly, if at all. But it had the bones of what we needed: a digital classroom where students could access materials, submit work, and communicate with teachers on their own schedule.

I made the call: Schoology would be our school. Not a supplement—the structure.

But I didn't mandate it. I brought it to my team—and then I brought it to Rita.

The Partnership That Saved Us

Rita and I had been meeting weekly for months by this point. We'd built trust. She knew I didn't make decisions in a vacuum, and I knew she'd fight for her teachers if I asked for something unreasonable.

I laid it out for her: "Rita, I think we're about to go remote. I don't know when, but I think it's coming. If we wait until the district tells us what to do, we'll be scrambling. I want to build the system now, with teacher input, so we're ready."

She was quiet for a moment. Then: "What do you need from me?"

"Help me build it. Work with your teachers. We need a consistent structure across all classes—same routine, same expectations—so parents and kids aren't learning six different systems. I need you to make sure this doesn't burn teachers out before we even start."

Over the next week, Rita and I worked with department leads to design the framework:

Every class would follow the same weekly rhythm: Monday overview, daily assignments posted by 8 a.m., office hours via Zoom twice a week

Assignments would be posted in Schoology with clear deadlines

Teachers would respond to student questions within 24 hours

Screen-time expectations would be limited—no more than 2–3 hours of direct instruction per day

Then we trained. We brought teachers in after school and walked them through Schoology step by step. We created templates, troubleshot tech issues, and answered the same questions a dozen times.

Critically, we planned our parent communication. We knew families would panic, so we designed a parent meeting in advance—not a passive webinar, but an interactive session using Zoom breakout rooms where parents could meet with departments, ask questions, and understand how the system worked.

We had it all mapped out a week before the shutdown was even announced.

When the official order came two weeks later, we were ready.

The Shutdown: When Preparation Met Crisis

March, 2020, the order came down: schools would close indefinitely.

Other schools scrambled. Teachers panicked. Parents flooded inboxes. District offices were overwhelmed.

We executed our plan.

Monday morning, our students logged into Schoology and found their classes waiting. Teachers posted assignments. Students submitted work. The system we'd built was live.

That same week, we held the parent meeting we'd planned in advance. Using Zoom breakout rooms, we divided families by department so they could meet directly with their students' teachers. Parents could ask specific questions, see how Schoology worked in real time, and understand exactly what their kids would be doing each day.

Over 600 families attended. We walked them through the system, answered questions, and reassured them: We've got this. Your kids are going to be okay.

The panic that consumed other schools? We didn't have it. Not because we were smarter, but because we'd prepared before the crisis hit.

That Monday, nearly 80% of our students logged in and submitted at least one assignment—a number that grew each week as families adjusted.

It wasn't perfect, but it was proof that readiness beats reaction every time.

The Wednesday Decision: When Good Strategy Meets Pushback

Ten days into remote learning, I made a change that sparked resistance: I adjusted the Wednesday schedule.

Instead of holding regular classes on Wednesdays, we created an Advisor/Office Hours day. During advisor time, teachers held online activities—team building, games, check-ins—anything that built connection without academic pressure. The rest of the day, teachers held office hours where students could drop in for help, ask questions, or just talk.

The pushback came immediately.

"We're losing instructional time," some teachers argued. "Students need content, not games."

Parents emailed: "Why aren't you teaching on Wednesdays? My child is falling behind."

Even some of my leadership team questioned it: "Can we really afford to give up a full day of instruction?"

I held firm. Here's why:

Teacher capacity. Five straight days of Zoom instruction wasn't sustainable. Teachers needed space to plan, respond, and recover.

Student safety. Advisor time gave every kid a weekly adult check-in. Increased isolation meant increased risk—abuse, neglect, mental health crises.

Engagement signal. Some students skipped class but showed up for advisor. That told us their struggle wasn't academic—it was emotional.

I brought the data to Rita and the teaching team. "Look at the attendance patterns. We're reaching kids on Wednesdays we're losing the rest of the week. This isn't a break—it's a different kind of learning."

When I shared the evidence, resistance faded—not from pressure, but from proof.

By the end of the first month, Wednesdays became the heartbeat of our week. Teachers used advisor time creatively—virtual talent shows, cooking competitions, read-alouds, student-led discussions. It wasn't wasted time. It was the glue holding everything together.

Learning to Live in the Long Haul

As weeks became months, we realized students needed more than schoolwork—they needed connection.

So we expanded. We hosted online game nights—trivia, Pictionary, Among Us tournaments. We held movie nights where students chatted in real time. We created virtual clubs. We celebrated birthdays over Zoom.

It wasn't the same as being together in person, but it was something. It reminded students that school was more than assignments—it was community.

By summer, it was clear: we weren't going back to normal in the fall.

We took what we'd learned in the spring and refined it. We improved our Schoology structure, trained teachers more deeply, and expanded tech support for families.

While other districts were still fighting over whether to reopen, we'd already moved past that debate. We knew what we were doing—and we knew why.

Strategic Takeaways for Leaders

Read weak signals before they become loud alarms. The best crisis leaders don't wait for official orders or clear mandates. They pay attention to early indicators—changes in tone, patterns in other industries, gut feelings that something's shifting. My wife's corporate shutdown was a weak signal. Acting on it gave us a two-week head start that made all the difference.

Decide with incomplete information. You'll never have perfect clarity in a crisis. If you wait until you're certain, you've waited too long. Make the best decision you can with what you know, then adjust as you learn more. I didn't know if schools would close—but I acted like they would.

Build systems, not heroics. Crisis leadership isn't about being the hero who saves the day. It's about creating systems that function when you're not there. Schoology became our system—reliable, predictable, scalable. It didn't require me to make a thousand individual decisions every day.

Use the alliances you've built. The partnership I'd cultivated with Rita paid off here. Because we'd built trust over months of weekly meetings, she didn't fight me—she helped me. You can't build that trust in a crisis. You have to build it before.

Communicate early and often. Panic spreads in the absence of information. We held parent meetings, sent regular updates, and over-communicated throughout the year. Parents knew what to expect, and that prevented the fear-driven chaos that paralyzed other schools.

Preparation is 90% of crisis leadership. The crisis itself is often short. But the preparation—the systems, the relationships, the trust—takes months or years to build. Sun Tzu was right: the skillful leader cultivates the situation before the crisis arrives.

The Deeper Lesson

In the military, we had a saying: "Prior planning prevents poor performance." Not poetic, but true.

The reason we survived COVID wasn't brilliant decisions under pressure—it was the boring work done ahead of time:

Building a relationship with the union so we could move fast when it mattered

Investing in technology infrastructure before we needed it

Training teachers on systems before the crisis hit

Establishing communication channels with families before panic set in

When the crisis came, we didn't invent solutions—we executed them.

Sun Tzu warned that desperate ground forces courage—but wise leaders shape the ground before the battle begins.

Yes, when you're in crisis, you must fight—but the real art of leadership is ensuring you're never truly desperate because you saw it coming and prepared accordingly.

Crisis doesn't reveal character. It reveals preparation.

Reflection Questions

What weak signals are you seeing right now that might indicate a future crisis?

Do you have systems that can function under extreme pressure, or are you relying on individual heroics?

Who are your key allies in a crisis, and have you built enough trust to move quickly with them?

Conclusion
Winning Smarter

The Strategic Path Forward

It's 8:00 AM on a Monday, and I'm back in a school hallway—not as a young principal trying to prove something, not as an outsider walking into a wounded building, but as a leader who has seen enough battles to know what really matters.

Students stream in with backpacks half-zipped, hoodies over their heads, and that early-morning mix of calm and chaos. A teacher hustles past, coffee in hand, already behind. Two students start jawing at each other near the lockers. And just like always, I slide into the moment—steady, present, reading the terrain, shaping the outcome before it even starts.

Command presence. Not about power. Not about intimidation. Just clarity in motion.

All these years later, I can tell you something with complete confidence:

School leadership has nothing to do with fighting harder. It has everything to do with thinking smarter.

And that's where Sun Tzu's wisdom becomes more than philosophy—it becomes a practical guide for surviving and leading in one of the most demanding professions in America.

What It All Comes Down To

Across these chapters, you've seen a pattern:

1. **Strategy before action**—Build plans before crises hit. Gather intelligence. Study your competition. Make calculations in the temple before the battle begins.

2. **Alliances over confrontation**—Influence works through relationships, trust, and respect. You don't win by overpowering people. You win by partnering with them.

3. **Energy as a finite resource**—Leaders who drain their people lose their people. Leaders who protect their people multiply their strength.

4. **Systems that outlast you**—Great schools aren't built on heroics. They're built on structures that continue when you're sick, on vacation, or gone for good.

5. **Know your terrain**—Every school is a living ecosystem. If you don't understand its culture, history, and informal power, you will step into battles you never needed to fight.

6. **Maneuver wisely**—Sometimes the direct approach fails. Sometimes the win comes from the move nobody expects—the indirect path that shifts the entire situation.

These aren't abstract ideas. They are practical tools—tools you can use tomorrow morning.

The Real Art of Leadership

People think strategy is cold and tactical. But real strategy—real Sun Tzu-level thinking—is actually an act of care.

It says:

I will plan so you don't burn out.

I will build systems so you don't have to survive chaos.

I will communicate clearly so you aren't blindsided.

I will create conditions where you can do your best work.

I will protect you from battles that don't need to be fought.

That's not war. That's leadership of the highest form.

And it's what your staff needs from you more than anything else.

What This Means for You

Whether you're new to the role or trying to rediscover the joy after years of pressure—you now have a different way of operating:

You don't have to react to everything.

You don't have to fight every battle.

You don't have to carry the school on your shoulders.

You can think strategically, lead with calm, move with intention, and create a school where the adults and the students can thrive.

Leadership stops feeling like survival when you stop playing checkers and start playing chess.

A Final Word

At the beginning of this book, I stood in a hallway and framed school leadership as a battlefield.

Not because students are the enemy.

Not because teachers are obstacles.

Not because parents are opponents.

But because leadership requires clarity, discipline, preparation, and courage.

Sun Tzu wrote:

"Supreme excellence consists in breaking the enemy's resistance without fighting."

In our world, the "enemy" is: chaos, burnout, dysfunction, broken systems, outdated thinking, weak communication, and the pressure that never lets up.

You defeat those forces not by working yourself into exhaustion... but by leading with intelligence, humility, and purpose.

You've spent this book learning how to do exactly that.

So wherever you go tomorrow—hallway, classroom, staff meeting, crisis, or calm—remember this:

True leadership isn't about fighting harder.

It's about winning smarter.

Now you know how.

About The Author

Darren L. Avent Sr. is a United States Marine Corps veteran who served eight years as an Amphibious Assault Vehicle Crewman, deploying to Desert Shield and Desert Storm. After reaching the rank of Corporal, he commissioned as an Infantry Officer in the Army National Guard, where the military funded his teaching credential and launched his transition into education.

Darren spent over a decade as a school principal in Oakland, California. He led transformations at Kaiser Elementary and Montera Middle School, building systems before they were needed and securing alliances before crises hit—the strategic approach he learned in the Marines.

Through Strategic Ed Leadership, Darren works with burned-out principals who are ready to move from reactive firefighting to sustainable, strategic systems. If you'd like to explore working together, visit strategicedleadership.com.

Darren lives in the Bay Area with his wife, who has supported him through every career transition and every late-night revision of this book.

Continue the Conversation

If this book helped you think differently about leadership, let's talk about what's next.

I work with principals who are ready to stop firefighting and start leading strategically. Through one-on-one coaching and group cohorts, I help school leaders build sustainable systems—without burning out.

Strategic Leadership Coaching – One-on-one partnerships for principals who want to build long-term capacity, not just survive the crisis.

Crisis Leadership Intensives – Focused support when you're facing immediate challenges: enrollment decline, staff conflict, community backlash, or sudden transitions.

Principal Cohorts – Small-group coaching for leaders who want to learn strategy alongside peers facing similar battles.

This isn't motivational speaking. It's strategic thinking applied to the real challenges you face every day.

Let's Talk

StrategicEd Leadership
strategicedleadership@gmail.com
strategicedleadership.com

Want to explore what strategic coaching could look like for you or your team? Reach out. Let's figure out how you can win smarter, not work harder.

www.ingramcontent.com/pod-product-compliance
Lightning Source LLC
Chambersburg PA
CBHW020753130626
46554CB00006B/2170